The Power of the
369
METHOD

**Unlock the Cosmic Code and Create the Life
you Desire using the Law of Attraction**

Sarah Ripley

The Power of the 369 Method

Copyright © 2023 Sarah Ripley & Street Cat Publishing

All rights reserved.

Other Titles by
Sarah Ripley

The 369 Project: A Manifestation Journal to Create the Life You Desire

The Shadow Work Journal: A Guide for Exploring your Hidden Self

101 Questions to ask Before you say "I Do"

The Lucky Girl Journal: A Guided Workbook for Manifesting your Dreams

Questions For Couples: 365 Questions to guide you to Stronger Communication, Trust and Intimacy

365 Daily AffirmationsFor Women: A Year fo Daily Affirmations to bring Peace, Joy and Happiness to your Life.

The Self-Love Workbook for Women: 90 Days to a More Loving and Accepting Relationship with Yourself

The Angel Numbers Book: Unlocking the Meaning and Divine Messages of Number Sequences

Exclusive Bonus Content to Amplify your Manifesting Power.

Scan the QR code to receive your FREE 33 Day Manifestation Tracker and Vision Board!

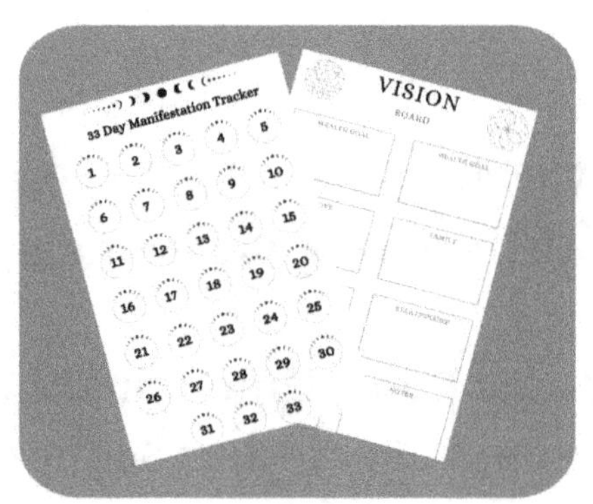

Table of Contents

The Symphony of Manifestation: Why 3, 6, and 9 Hold the Key to the Universe.

Nikola Tesla, the visionary inventor, once uttered a cryptic yet intriguing statement: "If you only knew the magnificence of the 3, 6, and 9, then you would have a key to the universe." These enigmatic numbers, woven into the fabric of his 3-6-9 manifestation practice, have sparked curiosity and debate for decades. But what truly lies behind their significance?

Imagine the number 3 as a bridge, gracefully arching between your individual consciousness and the boundless energy of the cosmos. In many cultures, three symbolizes completion, creation, and the divine trinity. For Tesla, it represented the direct link to the "Source," the universal force that governs all existence. By focusing on the number 3, you open yourself to this cosmic reservoir of power, paving the way for manifestation.

Think of the number 6 as a hidden vault, unlocking the depths of your own potential. In numerology, 6 is associated with balance, harmony, and responsibility. For Tesla, it signified the deep well of strength hidden within each individual. By repeating the number 6, you tap into this internal reservoir of resilience, courage, and determination, empowering you to overcome obstacles and push through limitations on your path to manifestation.

"If you only knew the magnificence of the 3, 6, and 9, then you would have a key to the universe."

- Nikola Tesla

Picture the number 9 as a phoenix rising from its ashes, representing transformation and renewal. In numerology, 9 symbolizes completion, compassion, and letting go. For Tesla, it signified the act of releasing the baggage of the past, including self-doubt, negativity, and limiting beliefs. By focusing on the number 9, you clear the emotional clutter that impedes your progress, allowing you to step into a fresh cycle of possibility and pave the way for your desires to manifest.

The Power of the 369 Method lies not just in the individual numbers, but in their harmonious orchestration. Repeating affirmations throughout the day creates a rhythmic resonance, tuning your mind to the frequency of the universe. It's like playing a cosmic melody, attracting your desires into existence through the power of focused intention and unwavering belief.

Remember, the true key to unlocking the universe lies not just in understanding the numbers, but in embodying their essence. Embrace the connection to the Source, harness your inner strength, and release any negativity that holds you back. With dedication and practice, the 369 Method can become a powerful tool for shaping your reality and manifesting your deepest desires.

Tesla's Trinity: Unveiling the Cosmic Code of 3, 6, and 9

While Nikola Tesla's name is synonymous with electrifying ingenuity and world-altering inventions, a lesser-known facet of his mind delved into the mysterious realm of numbers and their enigmatic connection to the universe. Beyond the hum of generators and the crackle of lightning, Tesla held a deep fascination with the trio of 3, 6, and 9, believing they represented the fundamental building blocks of existence itself.

Beyond the veil of our three-dimensional reality, Tesla believed, lay a higher plane. This realm, vibrated by the whispers of the unknown, held the key to understanding all existence. It was a symphony of numbers, and 3, 6, and 9 were the master chords, humming with potent energy.

In Tesla's eyes, these digits weren't mere numbers. They were potent keys, unlocking the very structure of matter, the flow of energy, and the language of frequency. His theory of 369 revolved around the concept of reducing any number to its essence by summing its individual digits. For example, 369 reduces to 9 (3+6+9=18 , 1+8=9) .For Tesla, these three numbers reigned supreme, holding the secret language through which all other numbers could be understood and interpreted.

The most captivating aspect of his theory lies in its connection to the very essence of existence: energy and frequency. He believed that 3, 6, and 9 were the only numbers that could exist as pure energy, retaining their identity even in the subatomic realm. This concept resonates with modern physics, where these numbers play a crucial role in understanding the dance of particles and the invisible forces that govern the universe.

Tesla's fascination wasn't confined to the sterile laboratory. He saw echoes of his 3-6-9 code in ancient philosophies, in the sacred number 108 of Hinduism and Buddhism, which also distills to 9 in his system. This connection suggests a deeper truth, a universal language woven into the fabric of human consciousness across time and cultures.

Tesla's 3, 6, and 9 weren't just numbers; they were a cosmic code, a hidden language whispering the secrets of the universe. By understanding them, by resonating with their frequencies, we unlock the potential to shape our reality, to dance with the unseen forces that govern all existence.

Think of the simple act of doubling numbers called the "Vortex Pattern". Start with 1, doubled it becomes 2, then 2 doubles to 4, then 4 to 8 to 16... This seemingly mundane sequence unfolds like a closed loop, never gracing the presence of 3, 6, or 9. It's as if these numbers exist in a different rhythm, a different dimension. Scientist Marko Rodin's concept of a "flux field" beautifully captures this idea, suggesting that 3, 6, and 9 represent a bridge, a vector from the familiar three-dimensional realm we live in to the uncharted territory beyond.

The significance of threes also ripples throughout human history, a cosmic echo resonating in ancient wisdom and modern science. The humble triangle, with its three sides, forms the base of pyramids, monuments reaching towards the heavens. Trinities, sacred trios signifying balance and completion, appear in countless cultures, from the "Father, Son, and Holy Ghost" of Christianity to the three jewels of Hinduism.

Even Tesla, the master of electricity and magnetism, found solace in the trinity of "energy, frequency, and vibration." He once said "If you want to find the secrets of the universe, think in terms of energy, frequency and vibration." Tesla believed these three fundamental forces held the key to unlocking the universe's hidden secrets, the unseen gears that turn the vast cosmic clock.

"If you want to find the secrets of the universe, think in terms of energy, frequency and vibration."

- Nikola Tesla

Perhaps the exclusion of 3, 6, and 9 in the simple doubling sequence isn't a void, but an invitation. It beckons us to look beyond the confines of our familiar dimension, to seek the hidden patterns woven into the fabric of reality. Could these enigmatic numbers act as stepping stones, guiding us towards the elusive "flux field," a pathway to a universe veiled from our everyday perception?

This is not just a theory; it's a call to action. Experiment with the numbers 3, 6, and 9. Feel their vibrations in your mind, their echoes in your soul. Let them be your guide, your key to unlocking the universe's hidden potential. Remember, the greatest discoveries often lie not in the grand pronouncements, but in the quiet whispers of numbers, waiting to be deciphered.

The Law of Attraction: From Thought to Manifestation

Tesla believed in the power of the mind. He often spoke about the mind's vast potential and its ability to influence the physical world. He famously said, "The future belongs to those who believe in the beauty of their dreams." This belief in the mind's power resonates with the core tenet of the Law of Attraction that our thoughts and beliefs shape our reality.

The Law of Attraction is a philosophy stating that our thoughts have a direct impact on our experiences. Put simply, what we focus on expands in our lives. This idea isn't just wishful thinking; it's based on the belief that our thoughts carry a specific energy. When we cultivate positive thoughts and emotions, we project that energy outward, attracting experiences that resonate on the same frequency. Conversely, negative thoughts emit a different energy, potentially drawing in undesirable circumstances.

The Law of Attraction is often described through three central principles:

1. Like Attracts Like: This principle suggests that similar things draw upon each other. It applies not just to relationships but also to the outcomes we attract. Focusing on positivity, optimism, and

"The future belongs
to those who believe
in the beauty of their
dreams."

- Nikola Tesla

gratitude helps us attract experiences that reflect those states. Conversely, dwelling on negativity or fear can potentially manifest undesirable results.

2. Filling the Void: The idea behind this principle is that our minds and lives naturally resist emptiness. When we remove negativity, we create space for something else to fill it. Proponents of this philosophy encourage actively cultivating positive thoughts and emotions to ensure that what fills that space aligns with our desired experiences.

3. The Power of the Present: This principle emphasizes the importance of focusing on the present moment. While challenges and disappointments may arise, the Law of Attraction suggests that within every difficulty lies an opportunity. By shifting our focus towards finding solutions, expressing gratitude for what we do have, and actively enjoying the present moment, we open ourselves to positive possibilities that may have been obscured by negativity.

Remember, The Law of Attraction is not a magic formula or a guarantee of instant success. It's a tool for conscious living, encouraging us to take responsibility for our thoughts and how they shape our experiences. By actively cultivating positive thoughts and aligning our energy with our desires, we can increase the likelihood of attracting experiences that reflect our highest aspirations.

The Law of Vibration: Understanding the Universe's Movements

Nikola Tesla saw the universe as a symphony of frequencies and vibrations. He believed that within this symphony lay the power to sculpt reality itself. Every thought, every object, hummed with its own unique tune, and by aligning with the right melody, one could manifest their desires. "Everything is a vibration," Tesla once declared, echoing the very essence of his transformative perspective.

The Law of Vibration proposes that everything in the universe, from the subatomic particles to the vast expanse of galaxies, exists in a state of constant movement and energy exchange. This movement, often referred to as vibration, takes the form of oscillations at specific frequencies. The rate at which something vibrates, its frequency, is its unique fingerprint in the energetic tapestry of the universe.

This vibrant symphony encompasses everything we perceive. A seemingly solid brick wall, for example, isn't truly static; its atoms and molecules are in constant, albeit slow, motion. In contrast, our bodies hum with a much higher vibrancy, a complex orchestra of cells and energy pulsating at significantly faster rates.

"Everything is a
vibration,"

- Nikola Tesla

The Law of Vibration isn't limited to the physical realm. Our thoughts, too, are forms of energy, each resonating at a distinct frequency influenced by their nature. A joyful thought, a burst of pure excitement, vibrates at a far higher frequency than the sluggish hum of anger or fear. These mental vibrations ripple through our internal landscape, impacting our emotional state and potentially even influencing the world around us.

This is where the Law of Vibration truly empowers us. We, as the conductors of our own internal orchestra, have the ability to choose the frequency we broadcast. By consciously directing our thoughts and cultivating positive emotions, we can elevate our internal vibration, aligning ourselves with states of joy, gratitude, and abundance. Conversely, dwelling on negativity can lower our frequency, potentially attracting experiences that resonate with that disharmony.

The Law of Vibration suggests that we attract what we emanate. Just like tuning forks, objects and experiences resonate with frequencies similar to their own. When we radiate a high frequency of positivity, we open ourselves to opportunities and circumstances that reflect that vibrancy. Conversely, when we broadcast negativity, we might attract experiences that mirror that discordant energy.

The Law of Vibration serves as the fundamental principle behind the Law of Attraction. This means that our thoughts and emotions, each vibrating at their own unique frequency, combine to create our overall energetic signature. This signature then acts as a magnet, attracting experiences and circumstances that resonate at the same frequency.

While it's true that our thoughts influence our reality, it's more accurate to say that it's our overall vibrational state, formed by the combination of thoughts and emotions, that determines what we draw into our lives. Focusing solely on positive thoughts may not be enough if our emotional state contradicts them. Therefore, cultivating a positive emotional landscape alongside positive thinking becomes crucial for manifesting desired outcomes.

Sacred Geometry and the Fibonacci Sequence

Sacred geometry is a fascinating intersection of mathematics, nature, and spirituality that explores the fundamental building blocks of the universe and their connection to spirituality. It involves the study of specific shapes, patterns, and proportions believed to hold deep meaning and significance across various cultures and religions.

The connection between sacred geometry and nature is a fascinating and ancient one, dating back to early civilizations who saw mathematical patterns and geometric shapes as reflections of the universe's underlying order.

Specific shapes like circles, spirals, spheres, triangles, and hexagons appear repeatedly in natural structures, from snowflakes and spiderwebs to flower petals and animal cells. These shapes represent efficiency, stability, and growth, mirroring the principles held sacred in many geometric traditions.

Sacred geometry emphasizes specific proportions like the Golden Ratio and the Fibonacci sequence, often found in nature and considered aesthetically pleasing. These proportions are believed to create harmony, balance, and order, reflecting the underlying structure of the universe.

The Fibonacci sequence is a famous sequence of numbers where each number is the sum of the two preceding numbers. It starts like this: 0, 1, 1, 2, 3, 5, 8, 13, 21, 34, and so on. What makes this sequence so fascinating is its unexpected connection to nature and the universe.

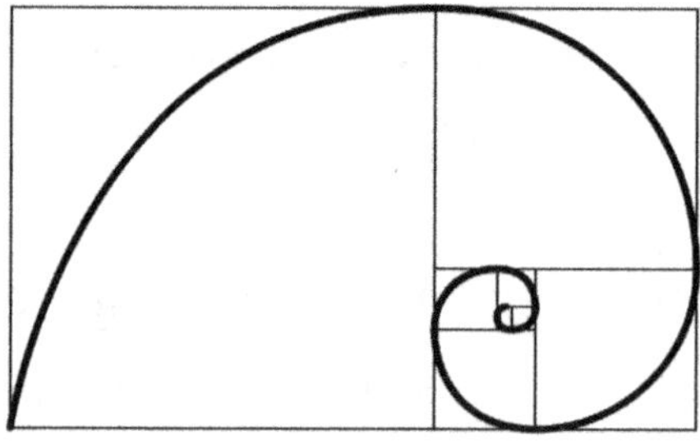

The Fibonacci sequence appears in countless spiral patterns in nature, from the nautilus shell and sunflower seed head to the arrangement of leaves on a stem. These spirals are often seen as symbols of growth and evolution, reflecting the sequence's self-repeating nature. The arms of many spiral galaxies, like our own Milky Way, follow a logarithmic spiral, mirroring the Fibonacci sequence in their growth and structure. This pattern might be related to efficient gravitational forces within the galaxy.

Trees, lungs and other branching structures often follow the Fibonacci sequence, with each branch splitting into two smaller branches, then four, then eight, and so on. This efficient branching pattern maximizes the surface area for capturing sunlight or nutrients.

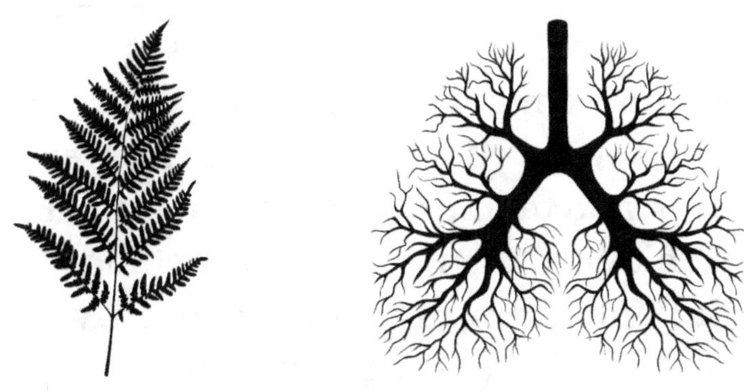

The Golden Ratio, derived from the Fibonacci sequence, is often found in the proportions of plants, animals, from flower petals to insect wings, and even human faces. This ratio is considered aesthetically pleasing and is often used in art and design.

The Fibonacci sequence, the Golden Ratio and Sacred Geometry represent fundamental principles of efficiency and optimization observed in natural systems. This suggests that these mathematical patterns are somehow "built-in" to the universe, influencing everything from the growth of a plant to the structure of a galaxy. These number sequences are a fascinating connection between mathematics, nature, and the cosmos and reminds us that everything in the universe is connected.

Manifesting: The Power to Bring Your Desires into Reality

Manifesting is the idea that you can attract your desires into your life through focused thoughts and intentions. At its heart, manifesting is about aligning your thoughts, emotions, and actions with your desires. It's about believing that you can create your own reality, and taking deliberate steps to make it happen. This doesn't mean simply wishing for something and hoping it appears magically. It requires effort, focus, and a willingness to put yourself out there.

The clearer you are about your desires, the easier it is to manifest them. Take some time to visualize your goals, write them down, and create a vision board to keep them at the forefront of your mind.

Your thoughts have power. Cultivate a positive mindset by focusing on what you want to achieve, rather than what you fear. Practice gratitude for what you already have, and visualize yourself succeeding.

You need to truly believe that you can achieve your desires. This unwavering faith is the fuel that powers manifestation. When doubt creeps in, remind yourself of your reasons for wanting something and why you deserve it.

Manifesting isn't passive. It requires taking inspired action towards your goals. This could involve networking, developing new skills, or putting yourself out there in new ways. Remember, the universe meets you halfway, but you need to take the first step.

Don't forget to be grateful for the small wins along the way. This not only keeps you motivated but also reinforces the positive energy you're putting out into the universe.

Affirmations are also a powerful tool for manifesting your desires. They work by planting positive seeds in your subconscious mind, which can eventually blossom into reality. Affirmations are positive statements repeated to reprogram your subconscious mind. By consistently voicing what you desire as if it's already true, you create a new belief system that can influence your thoughts, emotions, and ultimately, your actions.

Remember, Manifesting is a journey, not a destination. There will be ups and downs along the way. Don't get discouraged if your desires don't materialize overnight. Stay positive, persistent, and keep taking action. As you continue to practice, you'll find that your ability to manifest your desires grows stronger.

"The universe conspires with those who dare to manifest their desires,"

- Paulo Coelho

How to Use the 369 Method:

The 369 Method uses the power of repeated affirmations throughout the day and Aligned Actions to create the life you desire. By feeding your subconscious with unwavering belief, you can manifest anything you crave from the Universe.

Imagine your mind as a fertile garden. Every thought you plant takes root, growing into reality. The 369 Method is a powerful tool for cultivating the seeds of your desires. This isn't about wishful thinking; it's about harnessing the power of your subconscious mind, the hidden powerhouse behind your beliefs and actions.

Here's how it works:

- Plant your seeds: Choose a specific desire, something you truly crave. It could be anything from a new career to a healthier relationship, a creative breakthrough, or simply more joy in your life. Clearly define what you want to manifest, be it a specific goal, a feeling, or a situation. The more specific you are, the more focused your energy will be.

- Water them with affirmations: Throughout the day, at three specific times (morning, noon, and evening), write down your affirmation. Three times in the morning, six times in the afternoon and nine times at night. Write down a positive and concise statement that reflects your desire as if it has already manifested. Use present tense and avoid negative phrases. Instead of saying "I want to be healthy," say "I am healthy and full of energy." This repetition in the present tense helps your subconscious mind accept this new reality as true.

- Nurture with unwavering belief: Before starting the method, take a few deep breaths and set your intention to manifest your desire. This clarifies your purpose and strengthens your focus. Simply repeating the affirmations isn't enough. You must also cultivate genuine faith in your ability to manifest your desire. Visualize yourself already enjoying what you crave, feel the emotions that come with it, and let go of any doubts or fears.

- Think of the affirmations as sunlight, and your belief as water. With consistent care, your seeds of desire will sprout, growing stronger and more vibrant with each passing day. While writing your affirmations, visualize yourself already achieving your desire and focus on the feelings it would bring you. This emotional connection amplifies the power of your words. As your subconscious mind aligns with your conscious desire, the Universe starts to conspire in your favor, opening doors and aligning opportunities to help you achieve your goal.

The repetition schedule for your affirmations:

- Morning: As soon as you wake up, write down your chosen affirmation three times. Do this early before getting distracted by the day's activities.

- Afternoon: Choose a specific time in the afternoon, ideally around midday, to write your affirmation six times. Consistency in the timing helps build momentum and focus.

- Night: Before going to bed, write your affirmation nine times. This allows you to end the day on a positive note and plant the seeds of your desire in your subconscious mind.

Repeat this process for 33 days. Consistency is crucial for rewiring your subconscious mind and building momentum towards your manifestation. Don't skip days or let doubt creep in.

Remember, the 369 method is a tool to align your thoughts and intentions. It doesn't replace real-world action. Look for opportunities to align your actions with your desire and take inspired steps to make it happen. Aligned actions in the 369 method refer to steps you take in the physical world that are compatible and supportive of your desired manifestation. These actions aren't necessarily direct steps towards your goal, but they help create the circumstances and energy flow needed to attract it.

Aligned actions should resonate with your affirmation and reflect the kind of person you want to be in achieving your goal. For example, if your affirmation is "I am a confident and successful leader," aligned actions could be attending leadership workshops, networking with professionals in your field, or practicing assertive communication.

These actions put you in the right space to receive what you desire. They might involve joining relevant communities, putting yourself out there, or actively seeking information and resources that can move you closer to your goal.

But Don't overthink it! Aligned actions can be small and simple. Taking a walk in nature to clear your head, reading a book that inspires you, or simply expressing gratitude for the progress you've made can all be powerful forms of aligned action. Focus on feeling good and taking steps that resonate with your desired reality. Trust that the universe will respond to your energy and guide you towards what you're manifesting.

Remember, aligned actions are not about forcing outcomes or controlling the universe. They're about actively participating in your own manifestation journey, aligning your thoughts and actions with your desired reality, and trusting that the universe will support you on your path.

This 33-day ritual isn't just a scribbling exercise; it's a conversation with the universe and aligning your actions to create the life you desire. Each repetition amplifies the magnetic pull of your goals, like tuning forks vibrating at the same frequency. By actively engaging with your dreams, you're programming your subconscious mind to accept them as reality, dissolving your negative beliefs and paving the way for the manifestation of your dreams.

Remember, the 369 method is a journey, not a destination. It's about planting the seeds of intention and nurturing them with unwavering faith. Manifestation takes time and effort. Trust the process and be grateful for small wins and positive changes along the way. Focus on enjoying the journey and feeling good about your progress.

So, pick up your pen, breathe deeply, and let the rhythm of your desires guide your steps. Watch as your dreams, infused with intention and belief, blossom into vibrant realities.

How to use the Journal

Date *June 4th*

Today....

I am feeling:

Excited about my future

motivated

I will achieve:

checking off my "To do" list for the day

Making time for a walk today

meeting my deadline at work

I am looking forward to:

some "Me Time" after work

Giving my presentation at the meeting today

Trying a new healthy recipe for dinner

I am grateful for:

supportive friends

the beautiful city I live in

A job I love

MANIFEST
YOUR
DESIRE

Date _June 4th_

I Want To Manifest:

I have received a big promotion at work!

VISUALIZE
YOUR SUCCESS

How do I visualize this:

I have a large office

I have more self confidence

Respect of my peers

Financial security

Aligned Actions I will take today:

Be more efficient at work

Take a walk at lunch today to clear my thoughts

Network with my peers

ALIGNED
ACTIONS

AFFIRMATIONS

3 Morning Affirmations

I have received the promotion I deserve!

I have received the promotion I deserve!

I have received the promotion I deserve!

6 Afternoon Affirmations

I have received the promotion I deserve!

I have received the promotion I deserve!

I have received the promotion I deserve!

I have received the promotion I deserve!

I have received the promotion I deserve!

I have received the promotion I deserve!

9 Evening Affirmations

I have received the promotion I deserve!

I have received the promotion I deserve!

I have received the promotion I deserve!

I have received the promotion I deserve!

I have received the promotion I deserve!

I have received the promotion I deserve!

I have received the promotion I deserve!

I have received the promotion I deserve!

I have received the promotion I deserve!

My body is a vessel
for my soul, and I
treat it with respect
and kindness.

Today....

I am feeling:

____

____

____

I will achieve:

____

____

____

I am looking forward to:

____

____

____

I am grateful for:

____

____

Date ______

I Want To Manifest:

How do I visualize this:

Aligned Actions I will take today:

3 Morning Affirmations

6 Afternoon Affirmations

9 Evening Affirmations

I am grateful for the
love and support I
receive from my
loved ones.

Today....

I am feeling:

____

____

____

I will achieve:

____

____

____

I am looking forward to:

____

____

____

I am grateful for:

____

____

____

Date ________

I Want To Manifest:

____

How do I visualize this:

____

____

____

____

Aligned Actions I will take today:

____

____

____

____

3 Morning Affirmations

---

6 Afternoon Affirmations

---

9 Evening Affirmations

I am an infinite magnet for abundance and prosperity.

Today....

I am feeling:

____

____

____

I will achieve:

____

____

____

I am looking forward to:

____

____

____

I am grateful for:

____

____

Date ______

I Want To Manifest:

____

How do I visualize this:

____

____

____

____

Aligned Actions I will take today:

____

____

____

____

____

3 Morning Affirmations

____

____

____

6 Afternoon Affirmations

____

____

____

____

____

____

9 Evening Affirmations

____

____

____

____

____

____

____

____

____

I compare myself
only to my own past
self, not to others.

Today....

I am feeling:

____

____

____

I will achieve:

____

____

____

I am looking forward to:

____

____

____

I am grateful for:

____

____

Date _______

I Want To Manifest:

____

How do I visualize this:

____

____

____

____

____

Aligned Actions I will take today:

____

____

____

____

____

3 Morning Affirmations

---

6 Afternoon Affirmations

---

9 Evening Affirmations

I am constantly
learning and
evolving, and I am
excited to see who I
become.

Today....

I am feeling:

____

____

____

I will achieve:

____

____

____

I am looking forward to:

____

____

____

I am grateful for:

____

____

____

Date _______

I Want To Manifest:

____

How do I visualize this:

____

____

____

____

Aligned Actions I will take today:

____

____

____

____

3 Morning Affirmations

6 Afternoon Affirmations

9 Evening Affirmations

I am confident in my abilities, and I radiate that confidence in everything I do.

Today....

I am feeling:

____

____

____

I will achieve:

____

____

____

I am looking forward to:

____

____

____

I am grateful for:

____

____

____

I Want To Manifest:

____

How do I visualize this:

____

____

____

____

____

Aligned Actions I will take today:

____

____

____

____

____

3 Morning Affirmations

____

____

6 Afternoon Affirmations

____

____

____

____

9 Evening Affirmations

____

____

____

____

____

I am open to
receiving abundance
in all its forms,
material and
spiritual.

Today....

I am feeling:

____

____

____

I will achieve:

____

____

____

I am looking forward to:

____

____

____

I am grateful for:

____

____

I Want To Manifest:

____

How do I visualize this:

____

____

____

____

____

Aligned Actions I will take today:

____

____

____

____

____

3 Morning Affirmations

---

6 Afternoon Affirmations

---

9 Evening Affirmations

I release stress and negativity, and I welcome peace and joy into my life.

Today....

I am feeling:

____

____

____

I will achieve:

____

____

____

I am looking forward to:

____

____

____

I am grateful for:

____

____

____

Date ________

I Want To Manifest:

____

How do I visualize this:

____

____

____

____

____

Aligned Actions I will take today:

____

____

____

____

____

____

3 Morning Affirmations

____

____

6 Afternoon Affirmations

____

____

____

____

____

9 Evening Affirmations

____

____

____

____

____

____

I embrace my unique
voice and express
myself authentically,
without fear of
judgment.

Today....

Date _______

I am feeling:

____

____

____

I will achieve:

____

____

____

I am looking forward to:

____

____

____

I am grateful for:

____

____

Date _______

I Want To Manifest:

____

How do I visualize this:

____

____

____

____

Aligned Actions I will take today:

____

____

____

____

____

3 Morning Affirmations

____

____

____

6 Afternoon Affirmations

____

____

____

____

____

____

9 Evening Affirmations

____

____

____

____

____

____

____

____

____

I attract healthy and supportive relationships into my life.

Today....

I am feeling:

I will achieve:

I am looking forward to:

I am grateful for:

Date ________

I Want To Manifest:

____

How do I visualize this:

____

____

____

____

Aligned Actions I will take today:

____

____

____

____

____

3 Morning Affirmations

____

____

____

6 Afternoon Affirmations

____

____

____

____

____

9 Evening Affirmations

____

____

____

____

____

____

____

I am grateful for all
the good things in
my life, big and
small.

Today....

I am feeling:

____

____

____

I will achieve:

____

____

____

I am looking forward to:

____

____

____

I am grateful for:

____

____

I Want To Manifest:

____

How do I visualize this:

____

____

____

____

____

Aligned Actions I will take today:

____

____

____

____

____

3 Morning Affirmations

---

6 Afternoon Affirmations

---

9 Evening Affirmations

I am worthy of a
happy and fulfilling
life, and I create it for
myself.

Today....

Date _____

I am feeling:

____

____

____

I will achieve:

____

____

____

I am looking forward to:

____

____

____

I am grateful for:

____

____

Date ______

I Want To Manifest:

____

How do I visualize this:

____

____

____

____

____

Aligned Actions I will take today:

____

____

____

____

____

3 Morning Affirmations

---

6 Afternoon Affirmations

---

9 Evening Affirmations

I am guided by a
deep inner knowing
of my purpose.

Today....

I am feeling:

____

____

____

I will achieve:

____

____

____

I am looking forward to:

____

____

____

I am grateful for:

____

____

Date _______

I Want To Manifest:

____

How do I visualize this:

____

____

____

____

Aligned Actions I will take today:

____

____

____

____

____

3 Morning Affirmations

6 Afternoon Affirmations

9 Evening Affirmations

I celebrate my successes, big and small, and acknowledge my progress.

Today....

I am feeling:

____

____

____

I will achieve:

____

____

____

I am looking forward to:

____

____

____

I am grateful for:

____

____

I Want To Manifest:

____

How do I visualize this:

____

____

____

____

____

Aligned Actions I will take today:

____

____

____

____

____

____

3 Morning Affirmations

6 Afternoon Affirmations

9 Evening Affirmations

I am worthy of
feeling good in my
own skin.

Today....

I am feeling:

____

____

____

I will achieve:

____

____

____

I am looking forward to:

____

____

____

I am grateful for:

____

____

____

Date _______

I Want To Manifest:

____

How do I visualize this:

____

____

____

____

Aligned Actions I will take today:

____

____

____

____

____

3 Morning Affirmations

6 Afternoon Affirmations

9 Evening Affirmations

I am open to meeting
new people and
expanding my circle
of friends.

Today....

I am feeling:

____

____

____

I will achieve:

____

____

____

I am looking forward to:

____

____

____

I am grateful for:

____

____

____

Date ________

I Want To Manifest:

____

How do I visualize this:

____

____

____

____

Aligned Actions I will take today:

____

____

____

____

____

3 Morning Affirmations

---

6 Afternoon Affirmations

---

9 Evening Affirmations

I am open to
receiving guidance
and inspiration from
the universe.

Date _______

Today....

I am feeling:

____

____

____

I will achieve:

____

____

____

I am looking forward to:

____

____

____

I am grateful for:

____

____

Date ______

I Want To Manifest:

____

How do I visualize this:

____

____

____

____

____

Aligned Actions I will take today:

____

____

____

____

____

3 Morning Affirmations

6 Afternoon Affirmations

9 Evening Affirmations

I trust my intuition
and follow my
inspired ideas to
create wealth.

Today....

I am feeling:

____

____

____

I will achieve:

____

____

____

I am looking forward to:

____

____

____

I am grateful for:

____

____

____

Date ______

I Want To Manifest:

____

How do I visualize this:

____

____

____

____

Aligned Actions I will take today:

____

____

____

____

____

3 Morning Affirmations

____

____

____

6 Afternoon Affirmations

____

____

____

____

____

____

9 Evening Affirmations

____

____

____

____

____

____

____

____

I am open to new
ideas and
perspectives, and I
find inspiration in
the world around me.

Today....

I am feeling:

____

____

____

I will achieve:

____

____

____

I am looking forward to:

____

____

____

I am grateful for:

____

____

____

Date __________

I Want To Manifest:

____

How do I visualize this:

____

____

____

____

____

Aligned Actions I will take today:

____

____

____

____

____

____

3 Morning Affirmations

---

6 Afternoon Affirmations

---

9 Evening Affirmations

I listen to my body's
wisdom and honor
its needs.

Today....

I am feeling:

____

____

____

I will achieve:

____

____

____

I am looking forward to:

____

____

____

I am grateful for:

____

____

I Want To Manifest:

____

How do I visualize this:

____

____

____

____

Aligned Actions I will take today:

____

____

____

____

____

3 Morning Affirmations

6 Afternoon Affirmations

9 Evening Affirmations

My creativity flows
freely and
effortlessly, like a
vibrant river of
inspiration.

Today....

I am feeling:

____

____

____

I will achieve:

____

____

____

I am looking forward to:

____

____

____

I am grateful for:

____

____

____

Date _______

I Want To Manifest:

How do I visualize this:

Aligned Actions I will take today:

3 Morning Affirmations

---

6 Afternoon Affirmations

---

9 Evening Affirmations

I am surrounded by opportunities, and I am open to embracing them.

Date _______

Today....

I am feeling:

____

____

____

I will achieve:

____

____

____

I am looking forward to:

____

____

____

I am grateful for:

____

____

____

Date ______

I Want To Manifest:

____

How do I visualize this:

____

____

____

____

Aligned Actions I will take today:

____

____

____

____

3 Morning Affirmations

6 Afternoon Affirmations

9 Evening Affirmations

I am strong and capable of handling whatever life throws my way.

Date ________

Today....

I am feeling:

____

____

____

I will achieve:

____

____

____

I am looking forward to:

____

____

____

I am grateful for:

____

____

____

I Want To Manifest:

How do I visualize this:

Aligned Actions I will take today:

3 Morning Affirmations

6 Afternoon Affirmations

9 Evening Affirmations

I celebrate the
unique qualities of
each person in my
life.

Today....

I am feeling:

I will achieve:

I am looking forward to:

I am grateful for:

I Want To Manifest:

____

How do I visualize this:

____

____

____

____

Aligned Actions I will take today:

____

____

____

____

3 Morning Affirmations

---

6 Afternoon Affirmations

---

9 Evening Affirmations

I deserve wealth and
prosperity.

Date ______

Today....

I am feeling:

____

____

____

I will achieve:

____

____

____

I am looking forward to:

____

____

____

I am grateful for:

____

____

Date ____________

I Want To Manifest:

____

How do I visualize this:

____

____

____

____

Aligned Actions I will take today:

____

____

____

____

____

3 Morning Affirmations

6 Afternoon Affirmations

9 Evening Affirmations

I am capable of
achieving anything I
set my mind to.

Today....

Date ______

I am feeling:

____

____

____

I will achieve:

____

____

____

I am looking forward to:

____

____

____

I am grateful for:

____

____

Date _______

I Want To Manifest:

____

How do I visualize this:

____

____

____

____

Aligned Actions I will take today:

____

____

____

____

____

3 Morning Affirmations

6 Afternoon Affirmations

9 Evening Affirmations

My heart overflows
with gratitude for
the simple gifts of
life

Date ____

Today....

I am feeling:

I will achieve:

I am looking forward to:

I am grateful for:

Date ______

I Want To Manifest:

____

How do I visualize this:

____

____

____

____

Aligned Actions I will take today:

____

____

____

____

____

3 Morning Affirmations

6 Afternoon Affirmations

9 Evening Affirmations

I trust that the
universe has a plan
for me.

Date ______

Today....

I am feeling:

____

____

____

I will achieve:

____

____

____

I am looking forward to:

____

____

____

I am grateful for:

____

____

____

Date _______

I Want To Manifest:

____

How do I visualize this:

____

____

____

____

____

Aligned Actions I will take today:

____

____

____

____

____

3 Morning Affirmations

6 Afternoon Affirmations

9 Evening Affirmations

I am grateful for my unique gifts and talents.

Today....

I am feeling:

I will achieve:

I am looking forward to:

I am grateful for:

Date ______

I Want To Manifest:

____

How do I visualize this:

____

____

____

____

Aligned Actions I will take today:

____

____

____

____

____

3 Morning Affirmations

---

6 Afternoon Affirmations

---

9 Evening Affirmations

I trust that the
universe will bring
me the relationships
I need to grow and
learn.

Date _____

Today....

I am feeling:

____

____

____

I will achieve:

____

____

____

I am looking forward to:

____

____

____

I am grateful for:

____

____

I Want To Manifest:

____

How do I visualize this:

____

____

____

____

Aligned Actions I will take today:

____

____

____

____

3 Morning Affirmations

6 Afternoon Affirmations

9 Evening Affirmations

I trust my instincts
and believe in my
own judgment.

Today....

I am feeling:

____

____

____

I will achieve:

____

____

____

I am looking forward to:

____

____

____

I am grateful for:

____

____

Date ______

I Want To Manifest:

____

How do I visualize this:

____

____

____

____

____

Aligned Actions I will take today:

____

____

____

____

____

3 Morning Affirmations

---

6 Afternoon Affirmations

---

9 Evening Affirmations

I trust in the timing
of the universe, and I
know my purpose
will be revealed in
due time.

Today....

I am feeling:

____

____

____

I will achieve:

____

____

____

I am looking forward to:

____

____

____

I am grateful for:

____

____

____

Date _______

I Want To Manifest:

____

How do I visualize this:

____

____

____

____

Aligned Actions I will take today:

____

____

____

____

____

3 Morning Affirmations

---

6 Afternoon Affirmations

---

9 Evening Affirmations

I live a life of joy and gratitude, knowing that true prosperity lies in fulfillment and inner peace.

Today....

I am feeling:

____

____

____

I will achieve:

____

____

____

I am looking forward to:

____

____

____

I am grateful for:

____

____

3 Morning Affirmations

6 Afternoon Affirmations

9 Evening Affirmations

Your 369 Manifestation Journey

You've done it! Thirty-three days of potent 369 manifestation, a journey that has undoubtedly shifted your energy, ignited your desires, and whispered promises of the universe into your ear. Take a moment, dear reader, to bask in the accomplishment. You've unlocked a powerful tool, a secret language with the cosmos, and proven to yourself the power of unwavering belief.

This is not an ending, but a magnificent turning point. You've proven to yourself and the universe that you are a force to be reckoned with, a creator who can bend reality to your will. The vibrations you've sent out, the unwavering belief you've held, have reverberated through the cosmos. The universe heard you. It felt the fire of your passion, the unwavering certainty of your vision.

Now, as you step out of this 33-day crucible, remember this: the power of the 369 Method lies not just in the practice, but in the unwavering belief that carries it forward. The seeds you planted are sprouting, nourished by your tireless efforts. Trust the process. Continue to visualize your desires with laser-sharp focus. Speak them into existence with unwavering conviction. Take inspired action, guided by the whispers of your intuition.

Here are a few whispers to guide you on your continued journey:

- Embrace the ripple effect: Your 33 days have sent ripples of potent energy into the universe. Trust that these ripples are attracting your desires, even if they haven't yet materialized. Be patient, allow the universe to orchestrate its magic.

- Keep the fire burning: Don't let the embers of your 369 practice fade. Continue to write your desires, visualize them with vivid detail, and express gratitude for their arrival. Consistency is key in manifesting your dreams.

- Spread the word: Share your 369 experience with others. Inspire them to unlock their own power of manifestation. By sharing your story, you become a beacon, guiding others on the path to their own dreams.

Don't forget to celebrate your successes, big and small. Every manifested desire is a testament to your power. And when doubts creep in, remember the journey you've taken, the whispers of the universe you've heard, and the magic you've already unleashed. Keep manifesting, keep believing, and keep shining your light. The universe is waiting.

I hope all of your dreams
become reality. Hearing
your experience makes it
worth it

Scan the QR code to
leave a review for
The Power of the 369
Method

Preview the new Book by Sarah Ripley

Introduction

Angel Numbers: A Guide to Understanding the Messages Your Angels Are Sending You

In a world that often feels chaotic and uncertain, many people are seeking guidance and reassurance. Angel numbers, repeating sequences of numbers that are believed to be signs from angels or the universe, offer a way to connect with something greater than ourselves and find solace in the midst of life's challenges.

What are Angel Numbers?

Angel numbers are believed to be a form of divine communication, a way for angels or spirit guides to reach out to us and offer guidance, support, or encouragement. They can appear in a variety of ways, such as on clocks, license plates, phone numbers, or even in dreams.

If you are seeing angel numbers frequently, it may be a sign that celestial beings are trying to communicate with you. Pay attention to your thoughts and feelings when you see these numbers, as they may provide clues to the meaning of the message. You can also ask your angels or spirit guides for guidance on how to interpret the messages they are sending you.

~ 0 ~

The whispers of the Cosmos reach out to you, carried on the endless ring of Omega, a symbol of eternal potential. Be still, for within the silence, celestial beings offer guidance and reassurance.

~ 1 ~

Bask in the radiant light of your guiding spirits. Your thoughts, like seeds in fertile soil, sprout into reality. Trust in the loving embrace of your angels, and release your fears to the cosmic breeze.

~ 2 ~

The tapestry of your life unfolds with threads of celestial harmony. Let hope, a flickering flame, ignite your spirit, for the whispers of the Divine fan its embers.

~ 3 ~

Ancient wisdom, carried by angels who walk beside you, guides your path. Seek solace in the presence of a familiar spirit guide or a whisper of the Universe.

~ 4 ~

Feel the gentle brush of angel wings, a silent promise of support. Your prayers, like whispered wishes, ascend to the celestial realms, answered by the love and compassion of the Divine

~ 5 ~

The winds of transformation, orchestrated by the unseen hand of the Cosmos, dance around you. Embrace the change, for it leads to a brighter dawn. Call upon the celestial beings, and they will illuminate the path ahead.

~ 6 ~

Release your grasp on earthly desires, for your worth lies not in fleeting possessions, but in the boundless love of the Universe. Trust in the alchemists of the cosmos, who transmute worry into blessings.

~ 7 ~

Your journey unfolds on a path of grace, guided by the unseen hand of destiny. The magic of the Universe opens doors of opportunity like whispered secrets. Trust your intuition, for it is your celestial compass.

~ 8 ~

Abundance flows from the infinite wellspring of the Cosmos, its source the endless loops of the eight. Let this symbolize a boundless flow of blessings, aligning with your life purpose. Open your heart, and let the celestial bounty nourish you.

~ 9 ~

The celestial trumpet calls. The seeds of your purpose have ripened, and the harvest of action awaits. Take even the smallest step, guided by the unwavering support of your celestial companions.

~ 10 ~

Hold faith, for your thoughts are threads woven into the tapestry of your destiny. Let the celestial symphony of optimism resonate within you, for it is your guiding light to a future bathed in the golden light of the Universe.

~ 11 ~

Your thoughts manifest swiftly, Beloved. Focus on the good within you, others, and this situation, for positivity is the brush painting your reality. Stay optimistic,

~ 12 ~

The future echoes with the whispers of your thoughts. Keep faith and hope strong, for they are the threads weaving your destiny. Trust in the whispers of the Divine, guiding you towards a radiant future.

~ 13 ~

Ancient wisdom walks beside you. Spirit guides lend their light to your path. Embrace their guidance, and let their positive energy buoy your spirit.

~ 14 ~

Lean upon the wings of angels, child of the stars. They offer unwavering support, ensuring your optimism shines like a beacon in the darkness. Trust in their celestial embrace, and let your spirit soar.

~ 15 ~

Change dances around you, a whirlwind of possibility. Stay positive, for your optimistic thoughts are the seeds of manifestation. Embrace the transformation, and watch it blossom into your greatest good.

~ 16 ~

Your words, like whispered wishes, carry the power of creation. Be mindful, Beloved, for they are the magnets drawing your desires into reality. Speak with kindness, think with optimism, and watch the Universe align with your heart's song.

~ 17 ~

The celestial choir applauds your unwavering optimism! Your positive thoughts, like whispered prayers, paint your reality with vibrant hues. Keep the faith, for your path shines brightly ahead.

~ 18 ~

Your thoughts control the flow of abundance. Stay positive, and watch resources flow effortlessly towards you. Let go of worry, and trust in the angels' unwavering support. They guide you towards prosperity, hand in hand.

~ 19 ~

Believe in yourself for the Universe whispers your life purpose. The angels assure you – you are ready, equipped, and worthy. Let optimism be your compass, and take action with unwavering faith. Remember, you are a star, destined to shine.

About the Author

Sarah Ripley is a certified Life Coach, mentor, and author of books and journals on relationships, self-help, spirituality, and natural healing. She is also a trained Chakra healer, Naturopath, and Master Herbalist.

Sarah has a passion for helping others to live their best lives. She believes that we all have the power to heal ourselves and create the life we want. Her work is focused on helping people to connect with their inner wisdom and intuition, and to develop the tools and skills they need to live their lives in alignment with their values and purpose.

Sarah has traveled throughout Asia, South America and Europe studying different cultures and spiritual beliefs. She is also a nature lover who has done extensive trekking in the Himalayas, Rockies and Andes Mountains. She is a passionate advocate for natural living and enjoys cooking with a completely natural diet. She spends her free time relaxing with her family and cats.

Sarah has been married for 28 years and has 2 adult children. She currently lives in Southeast Asia with her husband and 4 adopted street cats, where she continues to write, teach, and mentor others. She is also working on a new book about her experiences with natural healing and spirituality.